MARGOT STARBUCK

365 Affirmations for Thriving Emotionally and Spiritually

Page composition by Charity Walton with Good Shepherd Publications at
www.goodshepherdpublications.com

Scripture quotations, unless otherwise noted, are from the New Revised
Standard Version of the Bible, copyright 1898 by the Division of Christian
Education of the National Council of the Churches of Christ in the USA.
Used by permission. All rights reserved.

Ordering Information:
Quantity sales. Special discounts are available on quantity purchases by cor-
porations, associations, and others. For details, contact the publisher by email
at wordmelon@gmail.com.

Printed in the United States of America

Publisher's Cataloging-in-Publication data
Starbuck, Margot.
The Solid Place: 365 Affirmations for Thriving Emotionally and Spiritually

ISBN 978-0-9897961-3-2, The Solid Place, Print Edition,
SECOND EDITION

Contents

About The Solid Place

Every day God invites each one of us to live into what is most true about ourselves, about others, and about God.

And yet our experiences along the journey—loss, pain, suffering, trauma—have bullied us into believing lies about who we are, who others are, and who God is.

Truth, though, sets us free.

We are liberated as we reject the lies we've believed and choose, instead, to claim what is most true about who we are, who others are, and who God is.

In the person of Jesus, we hear God's constant whisper, "I am the one who is with you and for you," and we recognize the face that does not fail.

This is the voice to listen to.

This is the face to trust.

Daily Rhythm

Morning:
Read the paragraph-long reflection corresponding with the day of the month.

Turn the page and read that month's affirmation.

If you're able, memorize the affirmation.

Through the day:
Hold the day's affirmation in your heart and mind.

Evening:
Releasing the day's affirmation back to God, give thanks for the particular way God's truth is transforming you.

Notice what God is speaking to your heart.

Noticing God's Presence

In the past, when others were not able to be *for* you, you feared that you were alone: unseen, unheard, unknown, and unloved. And so you carry with you the lingering suspicion that God is not with you and for you. But the One who can be trusted is not distracted or absent. Beloved, God is fully present to you in this moment and in all others. God sees you. God hears you. God knows you. God loves you. Aware of your past, your present, and your future, God sees what is hidden from others and even what is hidden from you. The One who loves you, and who is intimately familiar with your delicate places, is completely present to you. God is here now.

JAN 01

God is noticing me, right now.

"But even the hairs of your head are all counted. Do not be afraid; you are of more value than many sparrows." (Luke 12:7)

FEB 01

God is not preoccupied.

"From where he sits enthroned he watches all the inhabitants of the earth—he who fashions the hearts of them all, and observes all their deeds." (Psalm 33:14-15)

MAR 01

God knows the state I'm in.

"The eyes of the Lord are on the righteous, and his ears are open to their cry." (Psalm 34:15)

APR 01

God is aware of what I am not.

"For human ways are under the eyes of the Lord, and he examines all their paths." (Proverbs 5:21)

MAY 01

God knows my suffering.

"Many are the afflictions of the righteous, but the Lord rescues..." (Psalm 34:19)

JUN 01

I trust my creator with my most delicate places.

"For it was you who formed my inward parts; you knit me together in my mother's womb." (Psalm 139:13)

JUL 01

God is grieved by what I have suffered.

"You shall not abuse any widow or orphan. If you do abuse them, when they cry out to me, I will surely heed their cry." (Exodus 22:22-23)

AUG 01

The eyes of the compassionate one are on me.

"...while he was still far off, his father saw him and was filled with compassion; he ran and put his arms around him and kissed him." (Luke 15:20)

SEP 01

No moment of my journey has escaped God's notice.

"The eyes of the Lord are in every place, keeping watch on the evil and the good." (Proverbs 15:3)

OCT 01

God sees what others do not see.

"The Lord does not see as mortals see; they look on the outward appearance, but the Lord looks on the heart." (1 Samuel 16:7)

NOV 01

I want to be seen by others, but God's noticing is enough.

"I will exult and rejoice in your steadfast love, because you have seen my affliction; you have taken heed of my adversities." (Psalm 31:7)

DEC 01

When I've not been loved, God has seen.

"...the Lord saw that Leah was unloved...." (Genesis 29:31)

Releasing What is Not Yours

When you were undone, you clung to what you believed you could control to escape the discomfort of what you could not control. This is natural. But tight-fisted control has not served you well. So now, as you choose to live from the solid place, you are releasing what you once held tightly: pain, anxiety, worries, disappointment, defenses, obligations, blame, and your concern about the opinions of others. This choice to trust God requires tolerating a measure of discomfort. With a relaxed, secure, openhanded posture, you are choosing to relinquish that which is not yours to hold. When you choose to accept what you cannot change, you opt to trust God. Every time you release the wish that reality would be other than it is, you experience freedom.

JAN 02

I release obligation.

"But Peter and John answered them, 'Whether it is right in God's sight to listen to you rather than to God, you must judge.'" (Acts 4:19)

FEB 02

I trust God by letting go of the defenses I no longer need.

"I will give them one heart, and put a new spirit within them; I will remove the heart of stone from their flesh and give them a heart of flesh." (Ezekiel 11:19)

MAR 02

I lovingly release those who aren't the friends I need.

"For God did not give us a spirit of cowardice, but rather a spirit of power and of love and of self-discipline." (2 Timothy 1:7)

APR 02

As I release the opinion of others, I experience freedom.

"For they loved human glory more than the glory that comes from God." (John 12:43)

MAY 02

I release my cares to God in prayer.

"Do not worry about anything, but in everything by prayer and supplication with thanksgiving let your requests be made known to God." (Philippians 4:6)

JUN 02

I release the desire that life were different than it is.

"Cast your burden on the Lord, and he will sustain you; he will never permit the righteous to be moved." (Psalm 55:22)

JUL 02

I release what I do not or cannot know.

"And before him no creature is hidden, but all are naked and laid bare to the eyes of the one to whom we must render an account." *(Hebrews 4:13)*

AUG 02

I release thoughts and words about myself that are not true.

"I will restore health to you, and your wounds I will heal, says the Lord, because they have called you an outcast: 'It is Zion; no one cares for her.'" *(Jeremiah 30:17)*

SEP 02

I am not obligated to satisfy the demands of others.

"...we speak, not to please mortals, but to please God who tests our hearts." *(1 Thessalonians 2:4)*

OCT 02

I prayerfully release my disappointment in others.

"Even my bosom friend in whom I trusted, who ate of my bread, has lifted the heel against me." (Psalm 41:9)

NOV 02

I release what I cannot change.

"When I am afraid, I put my trust in you. In God, whose word I praise, in God I trust; I am not afraid; what can flesh do to me?" (Psalm 56:3-4)

DEC 02

Though releasing my pain feels scary, I entrust it to God.

"When the righteous cry for help, the Lord hears, and rescues them from all their troubles." (Psalm 34:17)

Understanding Your Worth

When your experience failed to confirm your inherent worth, you were tempted to believe the enemy's lie that you were not enough. In the absence of a reliable guiding voice, you naturally assumed that you deserved no more than you received. Graciously, you have been addressed by the voice that does not lie. This voice announces the reality that you are irrefutably worthy of love and respect, and that you are worth protecting and nurturing. Because God receives you as you are and not as you should be, you are discovering that in God's presence you need not be anything other than what you are. Whatever your condition today, there's nothing you can do to be more worthy of love than you already are. In this moment and all others, you are accepted and received by God.

JAN 03

Because I bear the divine image, I am irrefutably worthy.

"So God created humankind in his image; in the image of God he created them; male and female he created them." (Genesis 1:27)

FEB 03

I am, and always have been, worth respecting.

"Then God said, "Let us make humankind in our image, according to our likeness." (Genesis 1:26)

MAR 03

When I don't receive human love, I'm still worth loving. ·

"We know love by this, that he laid down his life for us—and we ought to lay down our lives for one another." (1 John 3:16)

APR 03

I am worth showing up for and sticking around for.

"I will not leave you orphaned; I am coming to you." (John 14:18)

MAY 03

I am, and have always been, worth protecting.

"The Lord is good, a stronghold in a day of trouble; he protects those who take refuge in him." (Nahum 1:7)

JUN 03

I am worthy of care.

"How much more valuable is a human being than a sheep!" (Matthew 12:12)

JUL 03

Nothing can make me more accepted than I already am.

"But the free gift of God is eternal life in Christ Jesus our Lord."
(Romans 6:23)

AUG 03

I am, and always have been, worth nurturing.

"Cast all your anxiety on him, because he cares for you."
(1 Peter 5:7)

SEP 03

When others do not accept me, I am received by God.

"...he has now reconciled in his fleshly body through death, so as to present you holy and blameless and irreproachable before him."
(Colossians 1:22)

OCT 03

I am enough.

"Look to him, and be radiant; so your faces shall never be ashamed." (Psalm 34:5)

NOV 03

I was meant to be.

"In your book were written all the days that were formed for me, when none of them as yet existed." (Psalm 139:16)

DEC 03

Made by God, I am worthy of love.

"Even the hairs of your head are all counted." (Matthew 10:30)

Accepting What Is

You suffered when you clung to the wish that what was should not have been. Or that what is should not be. But your dogged resistance has not brought you life. As you choose to accept that you cannot change what is—your past or the actions of others—you are being set free. And as you accept the fundamental reality of God's unfailing love for you, you are able to bear what is without anxiety. You imitate Jesus by changing what you can and accepting what you cannot. And, like Jesus, neither undoes you. As you choose to walk in the good way, you are discovering that you can allow what is without sinking. As you practice accepting what is, you flourish.

JAN 04

I accept the reality of God's love.

"And a voice from heaven said, 'This is my Son, the Beloved, with whom I am well pleased.'" (Matthew 3:17)

FEB 04

I can accept reality as it is and not be undone.

"I can do all things through him who strengthens me." (Philippians 4:13)

MAR 04

I choose to accept what is most true about God, about others, and about myself.

"Finally, beloved, whatever is true, whatever is honorable, whatever is just…think about these things." (Philippians 4:8)

APR 04

I change what I can and accept what I cannot change.

"But I trust in you, O Lord; I say, 'You are my God.'" (Psalm 31:14)

MAY 04

I dwell in the reality of Christ's belovedness and my own.

"You are my Son, the Beloved; with you I am well pleased." (Mark 1:11)

JUN 04

I accept the past I cannot change.

"We are afflicted in every way, but not crushed; perplexed, but not driven to despair..." (2 Corinthians 4:8)

JUL 04

With prayerful confidence, I accept what is.

"Father, if you are willing, remove this cup from me; yet, not my will but yours be done." (Luke 22:42)

AUG 04

I'm learning to accept parts of myself I once tried to hide.

"Search me, O God, and know my heart." (Psalm 139:23)

SEP 04

I can acknowledge my pain without sinking.

"When you pass through the waters, I will be with you; and through the rivers, they shall not overwhelm you..." (Isaiah 43:2a)

OCT 04

I accept those who aren't as I wish them to be.

"The Pharisees and their scribes were complaining to his disciples, saying, 'Why do you eat and drink with tax collectors and sinners?'" (Luke 5:30)

NOV 04

I flourish as I cling to God's love.

"But I am like a green olive tree in the house of God. I trust in the steadfast love of God forever and ever." (Psalm 52:8)

DEC 04

When I accept what is, it does not undo me.

"Trust in the Lord forever, for in the Lord God you have an everlasting rock." (Isaiah 26:4)

Recognizing God's Fidelity

The earliest human faces your life naturally prefigured your expectations of God. So when human faces failed— when your caregivers reflected sorrow, displeasure, contempt, or absence—you feared that God was not reliable. Although this is understandable, you are now discerning that the voice insisting that God has abandoned you is not the voice to trust. Instead, the voice that can be trusted confirms, "I am here now." In every moment, God is present with you. God sees. God hears. God knows. God cares. Even when you are where you do not want to be, God is faithfully present. God will not, and God cannot, abandon or forsake you. In every moment God gently whispers, "I am the one who is with you and for you." As you choose to stand in the solid place, you experience God's steadfast loving presence.

JAN 05

God hears me in every moment.

"I knew that you always hear me, but I have said this for the sake of the crowd standing here, so that they may believe that you sent me." (John 11:42)

FEB 05

God waits patiently with me in my loneliness.

"Even the darkness is not dark to you; the night is as bright as the day, for darkness is as light to you." (Psalm 139:12)

MAR 05

God is listening to me right now.

"But know that the Lord has set apart the faithful for himself; the Lord hears when I call to him." (Psalm 4:3)

APR 05

God receives my complaints, doubts, and objections.

"This poor soul cried, and was heard by the Lord, and was saved from every trouble." (Psalm 34:6)

MAY 05

God is faithful to listen.

"And this is the boldness we have in him, that if we ask anything according to his will, he hears us." (1 John 5:14)

JUN 05

God is with me even when I'm where I do not want to be.

"The Lord was with Joseph, and he became a successful man..." (Genesis 39:2)

JUL 05

God hears every desperate cry of my heart.

"Depart from me, all you workers of evil, for the Lord has heard the sound of my weeping." (Psalm 6:8)

AUG 05

God hears my prayer.

"But truly God has listened..." (Psalm 66:19)

SEP 05

God weeps with me.

"O that my head were a spring of water, and my eyes a fountain of tears, so that I might weep day and night for the slain of my poor people!" (Jeremiah 9:1)

OCT 05

In my bleakest moments, I have never been alone.

"Even though I walk through the darkest valley, I fear no evil;
for you are with me; your rod and your staff—they comfort me."
(Psalm 23:4)

NOV 05

God meets me exactly where I am.

"Those who are well have no need of a physician, but those who
are sick; I have come to call not the righteous but sinners." (Mark
2:17)

DEC 05

God hears me when I am in the pit.

"I called to the Lord out of my distress, and he answered me; out of
the belly of Sheol I cried, and you heard my voice." (Jonah 2:2)

Choosing the Good Way

When you were sinking you felt emotionally undone. But you are no longer bullied by your feelings or by the whims of others. Instead, you are choosing, in every moment, to live from the solid place. Today you can notice your feelings without being overwhelmed by them. You can accept the choices of others, even when they are not what you wish. Rejecting the story that is untrue, or partially true, you are choosing to embrace what is *most* true about you, about God, and about others. Every time ~~that~~ you choose thoughts that are life-giving, and release those that are death-dealing, you are being grounded more firmly in reality. As you choose daily for truth and life, you are being made well.

JAN 06

I lift my eyes from human faces to God's face.

"I will be a father to him, and he shall be a son to me..."
(2 Samuel 7:14)

FEB 06

I am journeying toward wholeness.

"When Jesus saw him lying there and knew that he had been there
a long time, he said to him, 'Do you want to be made well?'"
(John 5:6)

MAR 06

I choose to notice that God is always with me.

"And I will walk among you, and will be your God, and you shall
be my people." (Leviticus 26:12)

APR 06

I choose to remain in the light.

"In him was life, and the life was the light of all people."
(John 1:4)

MAY 06

I choose to stay tenderhearted.

"I will remove from your body the heart of stone and give you a
heart of flesh." (Ezekiel 36:26)

JUN 06

I choose to trust the words of Jesus.

"But these are written so that you may come to believe that Jesus is
the Messiah, the Son of God, and that through believing you may
have life in his name." (John 20:31)

JUL 06

As I make small choices for life, I am being made well.

"Now, discipline always seems painful rather than pleasant at the time, but later it yields the peaceful fruit of righteousness..." *(Hebrews 12:11)*

AUG 06

I didn't choose my suffering, but I choose to face it.

"I keep the Lord always before me; because he is at my right hand, I shall not be moved." (Psalm 16:8)

SEP 06

I choose satisfaction and joy.

"Though the flock is cut off from the fold, and there is no herd in the stalls, yet I will rejoice in the Lord..." (Habakkuk 3:17-18)

OCT 06

I choose to reject what is false.

"Resist the devil, and he will flee from you." (James 4:7)

NOV 06

I choose life by refusing to dwell on past hurts.

"Turn my eyes from looking at vanities; give me life in your ways." (Psalm 119:37)

DEC 06

I choose to release childish ways of perceiving the world.

"Brothers and sisters, do not be children in your thinking; rather, be infants in evil, but in thinking be adults." (1 Corinthians 14:20)

Affirming God's Graciousness

At some point, those you once needed most chose to be *for* themselves at your expense. Dubious about God's goodness and reliability, you have suspected that God has been like these ones. But you are discovering One who is like no other. In God's voice, love and truth are inextricably wed. You are coming to know, in your deepest places, that God is available now and is faithful to provide what you most need. You're learning that God can be trusted. God's countenance is turned toward you and God's heart toward you is kind. Whether or not you feel God's nearness, God's steadfast faithful love does not fail. In this moment, and in all others, God is with you and for you.

JAN 07

God is not the author of my suffering.

"...for he does not willingly afflict or grieve anyone." (Lamentations 3:33)

FEB 07

I trust the face that does not fail.

"It is the Lord who goes before you. He will be with you; he will not fail you or forsake you. Do not fear or be dismayed." (Deuteronomy 31:8)

MAR 07

God is healing the world, and God is healing me.

"I am the Lord who heals you." (Exodus 15:26)

APR 07

God is generous with me.

"He who supplies seed to the sower and bread for food will supply and multiply your seed for sowing." (2 Corinthians 9:10)

MAY 07

I am being transformed by God's kindness.

"Do you not realize that God's kindness is meant to lead you to repentance?" (Romans 2:4)

JUN 07

God's face and voice are available to me.

"'Come,' my heart says, 'seek his face!' Your face, Lord, do I seek." (Psalm 27:8)

JUL 07

God can be trusted.

"Now the angel of the Lord…said, 'I brought you up from Egypt, and brought you into the land that I had promised to your ancestors…'" (Judges 2:1)

AUG 07

God's face is gracious.

"The Lord bless you and keep you; the Lord make his face to shine upon you, and be gracious to you; the Lord lift up his countenance upon you, and give you peace." (Numbers 6:24-26)

SEP 07

God provides what I most need.

"Jesus said to them, 'I am the bread of life. Whoever comes to me will never be hungry, and whoever believes in me will never be thirsty.'" (John 6:35)

OCT 07

God is accessible.

"And I will never again hide my face from them, when I pour out my spirit upon the house of Israel, says the Lord God." (Ezekiel 29:29)

NOV 07

God's heart toward me is kind.

"The goodness and loving kindness of God our Savior appeared." (Titus 3:4)

DEC 07

The steadfast face of God shines on me.

"There are many who say, 'O that we might see some good! Let the light of your face shine on us, O Lord!'" (Psalm 4:6)

Inhabiting The Story That is True

Naturally, your story has shaped you. But when you were stuck, you were unable to interpret what was most true about yourself, about others, and about God. Now you have chosen to journey with the interpreter who offers meaning to your experience. With each step, God's Spirit is teaching you to live from the solid place. Today, walking in the reality of your inherent belovedness, you can tell your story without sinking because it no longer has power over you. As you embrace the story that is most real and most true, you are becoming increasingly aware of the presence of your faithful guide. And when you wander from the path, God's gentle whisper invites you to return to the solid place.

JAN 08

I don't have to orchestrate my own redemption.

"Our Redeemer—the LORD of hosts is his name—is the Holy One of Israel." (Isaiah 47:4)

FEB 08

My suffering matters, and has always mattered, to God.

"The Lord has been mindful of us." (Psalm 115:12)

MAR 08

I do not yet have the big picture, but I trust a loving God.

"I have said this to you, so that in me you may have peace. In the world you face persecution. But take courage; I have conquered the world!" (John 16:33)

APR 08

God interprets the meaning of my life story.

"You gave your good spirit to instruct them..." (Nehemiah 9:20)

MAY 08

I believe love is stronger than death.

"For God so loved the world that he gave his only Son, so that everyone who believes in him may not perish but may have eternal life." (John 3:16)

JUN 08

I was made to love and be loved.

"Be kind to one another, tenderhearted, forgiving one another, as God in Christ has forgiven you." (Ephesians 4:32)

JUL 08

In Jesus I discover what it is to be grounded in reality.

"Jesus increased in wisdom and in years, and in divine and human favor." (Luke 2:52)

AUG 08

God redeems the pieces of my story.

"Lo, your king comes to you; triumphant and victorious is he, humble and riding on a donkey, on a colt, the foal of a donkey." (Zechariah 9:9)

SEP 08

I speak only what is true of myself and others.

"Let no evil talk come out of your mouths, but only what is useful for building up." (Ephesians 4:29)

OCT 08

I discern when it's safe to share my story.

"Prudence will watch over you; and understanding will guard you." (Proverbs 2:11)

NOV 08

Death does not have the final word in my story.

"Set me as a seal upon your heart, as a seal upon your arm; for love is strong as death, passion fierce as the grave." (Song of Solomon 8:6)

DEC 08

I can trust that my story will end well.

"I am confident of this, that the one who began a good work among you will bring it to completion by the day of Jesus Christ." (Philippians 1:6)

Moving Beyond Your Past

There have been those on your journey who have offered you glimpses of God's steadfast, faithful love and others who have failed to do so. Under the Spirit's tutelage, you are learning to distinguish between the two. Because human faces fail, you have not received the fullness of love for which you were made and for which you naturally yearn. Out of that void, the voice that lies hisses that you deserved what you got. But this is not God's voice. God's voice says, "Your past does not define you. As I redeem what you have endured, you are being made new." Knowing what you have suffered, God receives every part of you. And though you need not forget the pain of your past, you are no longer bound by it. By God's grace, you are being set free.

JAN 09

Throughout my history, God has seen me.

"God looked upon the Israelites, and God took notice of them."
(Exodus 2:25)

FEB 09

Nothing done to me can change God's love for me.

"Though I walk in the midst of trouble, you preserve me against
the wrath of my enemies." (Psalm 138:7)

MAR 09

What I have endured does not define me.

"… have clothed yourselves with the new self, which is being re-
newed in knowledge according to the image of its creator." (Colos-
sians 3:10)

APR 09

Graciously, I'm being re-identified as God's own child.

"And I will say to Lo-ammi, * *'You are my people'; and he shall say, 'You are my God.'" (Hosea 2:23)   [*Lo-ammi means "not my people"]*

MAY 09

I don't forget my past, but I'm no longer bound by it.

"As servants of God, live as free people." (1 Peter 2:16)

JUN 09

In every moment, God knows my history and my hurts.

"Truly the eye of the Lord is on those who fear him, on those who hope in his steadfast love." (Psalm 33:18)

JUL 09

Jesus' wounds heal my wounds.

"He himself bore our sins in his body on the cross, so that, free from sins, we might live for righteousness; by his wounds you have been healed." (1 Peter 2:24)

AUG 09

Though human families fail, God's love does not fail.

"He will turn the hearts of parents to their children and the hearts of children to their parents..." (Malachi 4:6)

SEP 09

God knows the hurts I suffered before I had words.

"Upon you I have leaned from my birth; it was you who took me from my mother's womb. My praise is continually of you." (Psalm 71:6)

OCT 09

What others did not provide, I can now access.

"Fathers, do not provoke your children, or they may lose heart."
(Colossians 3:21)

NOV 09

When I suffer, God is near.

"The Lord is near to the brokenhearted, and saves the crushed in
spirit." (Psalm 34:18)

DEC 09

I release the old label; it doesn't describe who I really
am.

"In the place where it was said to them, 'You are not my people,' it
shall be said to them, 'Children of the living God.'" (Hosea 1:10)

Opting for Truth

You were once hoodwinked by the lies of the deceiver. Custom-fit to your experience, molded around the tiniest kernel of truth, yet twisted beyond recognition, these lies diminished you as they took root in your deepest places. They did not tell the truth about who you are and what you're worth. But as God's Spirit spoke truth to your mind and heart, you began to recognize each lie. This noticing, allowing you to reject what is false and to choose for what is most true, is a gift! Exposed, the deceiver's lies lose traction. Today you seize each lie that surfaces, recognizing it as an opportunity for freedom. You reject and replace the lies with what is most real and most true about you, about God, and about others. Clinging to God's truth, you walk in freedom.

JAN 10

My work is to choose truth.

"Lead me in your truth, and teach me, for you are the God of my salvation; for you I wait all day long." (Psalm 25:15)

FEB 10

My feelings do not, and cannot, alter God's truth.

"Think over what I say, for the Lord will give you understanding in all things." (2 Timothy 2:7)

MAR 10

I listen as God speaks truth to my heart.

"…the Spirit of truth…will guide you into all the truth" (John 16:13)

APR 10

I walk in truth.

"I have no greater joy than this, to hear that my children are walking in the truth." (3 John 1:4)

MAY 10

I reject the deceiver's lies, and listen for Christ's truth.

"...as the serpent deceived Eve by its cunning, your thoughts will be led astray from a sincere and pure devotion to Christ." (2 Corinthians 11:3)

JUN 10

As I follow Jesus, I walk in the way of truth.

"Jesus said to him, 'I am the way, and the truth, and the life. No one comes to the Father except through me.'" (John 14:6)

JUL 10

Every lie that surfaces is an opportunity for freedom.

"Sanctify them in the truth; your word is truth." (John 17:17)

AUG 10

As I submit to God's truth, I am transformed.

"Do not be conformed to this world, but be transformed by the renewing of your minds..." (Romans 12:2)

SEP 10

The truth sets me free and keeps me free.

"You will know the truth, and the truth will make you free." (John 8:32)

OCT 10

Rejecting what is hollow, I cling to what is solid and real.

"Set your minds on things that are above, not on things that are on earth." (Colossians 3:2)

NOV 10

I look to God's word, not to people, for truth and life.

"Turn away from mortals, who have only breath in their nostrils, for of what account are they?" (Isaiah 2:22)

DEC 10

I act on what I know to be true.

"Be strong and of good courage, and act. Do not be afraid or dismayed; for the Lord God, my God, is with you." (1 Chronicles 28:20)

Receiving God's Love

You once assumed that God's posture toward you would imitate what you had experienced in human relationships. This is natural. But you are discovering that God's love is of a different order than much of what you've encountered. God's steadfast love and faithfulness cannot fail. Even when you do not feel it, God's loving grip is sure. God is not someplace else; God is here. God is not for someone else at your expense; God is for you. God will not reject, forsake, or abandon you. In every moment you have access to the one who cares for you. Even in the darkest moments of your experience, nothing has, nothing can, and nothing ever will separate you from what is most real.

JAN 11

God is here now.

"Then Haggai, the messenger of the Lord, spoke to the people with the Lord's message, saying, I am with you, says the Lord." (Haggai 1:13)

FEB 11

God's sure grip on me doesn't depend on my awareness of it.

"Before I formed you in the womb I knew you, and before you were born I consecrated you; I appointed you a prophet to the nations." (Jeremiah 1:5)

MAR 11

I have never been alone.

"Yet it was you who took me from the womb; you kept me safe on my mother's breast." (Psalm 22:9)

APR 11

God cannot abandon me.

"We are afflicted in every way, but not crushed...persecuted, but not forsaken; struck down, but not destroyed." (2 Corinthians 4:8-9)

MAY 11

When I am afraid, God is with me.

"Do not fear, for I am with you." (Isaiah 43:5)

JUN 11

God is not somewhere else; God is here.

"And I will ask the Father, and he will give you another Advocate, to be with you forever." (John 14:16)

JUL 11

God is no less present in heartache than in joy.

"When they call to me, I will answer them; I will be with them in trouble, I will rescue them and honor them." (Psalm 91:15)

AUG 11

Nothing can separate me from the love of God.

"And remember, I am with you always, to the end of the age." (Matthew 28:20)

SEP 11

Right now, I have access to God.

"Draw near to God, and he will draw near to you." (James 4:8)

OCT 11

I can no longer be rejected or abandoned.

"No one shall be able to stand against you all the days of your life. As I was with Moses, so I will be with you; I will not fail you or forsake you." (Joshua 1:5)

NOV 11

Even when I don't feel it, God's love does not fail.

"The steadfast love of the Lord never ceases, his mercies never come to an end; they are new every morning; great is your faithfulness." (Lamentations 3:22-23)

DEC 11

I can be brave because I know I am not alone.

"I hereby command you: Be strong and courageous; do not be frightened or dismayed, for the Lord your God is with you wherever you go." (Joshua 1:9)

Navigating the Journey

When you were sinking, you were not holding on to what
was most true about you, about others, and about God.
You were pummeled by your feelings and burdened by
thoughts about your experiences. But you have chosen
to live from the solid place. Daily you choose to journey
with your reliable guide. You listen for the voice that can
be trusted and you set your eyes on the face that does not
fail. Brave, you confront what is. Wise, you notice your
thoughts, releasing those that do not bring life. Inten-
tional, you think and speak and act from the solid place.
Today, grounded in what is most real and true, you choose
to walk in the good way.

JAN 12

I listen for God's voice.

"He said to me: Mortal, all my words that I shall speak to you receive in your heart and hear with your ears." (Ezekiel 3:10)

FEB 12

I am expectant for what I can't yet see.

"Because we look not at what can be seen but at what cannot be seen; for what can be seen is temporary, but what cannot be seen is eternal." (2 Corinthians 4:18)

MAR 12

I accept that I may not understand what God is doing.

"For as the heavens are higher than the earth, so are my ways higher than your ways and my thoughts than your thoughts." (Isaiah 55:9)

APR 12

I choose what occupies my mind.

"We destroy arguments and every proud obstacle raised up against the knowledge of God, and we take every thought captive to obey Christ." (2 Corinthians 10:4-5)

MAY 12

I tip my gaze toward the face of Christ.

"...let us run with perseverance the race that is set before us, looking to Jesus the pioneer and perfecter of our faith..." (Hebrews 12:1-2)

JUN 12

I practice patience with others and myself.

"But if we hope for what we do not see, we wait for it with patience." (Romans 8:25)

JUL 12

I notice what God is doing in me.

"For it is God who is at work in you, enabling you both to will and to work for his good pleasure." (Philippians 2:13)

AUG 12

I choose to remain in God's love.

"Keep yourselves in the love of God." (Jude 1:21)

SEP 12

In each moment, I can exercise courage.

"If we live, we live to the Lord, and if we die, we die to the Lord; so then, whether we live or whether we die, we are the Lord's." (Romans 14:8)

OCT 12

Secure in God, I trust that the way out of unavoidable conflict is to go through it.

"When you walk through fire you shall not be burned, and the flame shall not consume you." (Isaiah 43:2)

NOV 12

I choose to be fully present in this moment.

"So do not worry about tomorrow, for tomorrow will bring worries of its own. Today's trouble is enough for today." (Matthew 6:34)

DEC 12

Although progress may be slow, God's presence is sure.

"You are my hiding place and my shield; I hope in your word." (Psalm 119:114)

Being Undone

When you were undone, you felt the sting of brokenness, pain, sin, and death. Naturally, you were tempted to find relief in that which promised to soothe. The deceiver even tried to convince you that you were responsible for your suffering, hissing: "You deserve this." "You're to blame." "You're not enough." But you know that this is not God's voice. God's voice says that you are resilient and well-equipped. Noticing you are stuck is an opportunity to offer your heart to God once again and find freedom. Because you are held in God's love, you can face all that is with the confidence that you will not be undone forever. You have all the resources you need to thrive.

JAN 13

When I am undone, I am not alone.

"Who will separate us from the love of Christ? Will hardship, or distress, or persecution, or famine, or nakedness, or peril, or sword?" (Romans 8:35)

FEB 13

I reject soothing substitutes and choose what is best.

"Why do you spend your money for that which is not bread, and your labor for that which does not satisfy?" (Isaiah 55:2)

MAR 13

My failing defenses make room for God's healing.

"He will cover you with his pinions, and under his wings you will find refuge; his faithfulness is a shield and buckler." (Psalm 91:4)

APR 13

I will not be stuck forever; God is at work in me.

"The Spirit of the Lord is upon me, because he has anointed me to bring good news to the poor. He has sent me to proclaim release to the captives." (Luke 4:18a)

MAY 13

My pain is a part of me, but it is not all of me.

"I consider that the sufferings of this present time are not worth comparing with the glory about to be revealed to us." (Romans 8:18)

JUN 13

Held in God's care, I lovingly face my wounds and scars.

"I sought the Lord, and he answered me, and delivered me from all my fears. (Psalm 34:4)

JUL 13

As I share my story, I offer to God whatever still hurts.

"Where, O death, is your sting?" (1 Corinthians 15:55)

AUG 13

Because blame keeps me stuck, I release it.

"The man said, 'The woman whom you gave to be with me, she gave me fruit from the tree, and I ate.'" (Genesis 3:12)

SEP 13

I won't be healed by my efforts, but by God's grace.

"O Lord my God, I cried to you for help, and you have healed me." (Psalm 30:2)

OCT 13

I may feel undone, but God is healing my heart.

"May the God of peace himself sanctify you entirely." (1 Thessalonians 5:23)

NOV 13

Noticing I am stuck is an opportunity to choose freedom.

"Heal me, O Lord, and I shall be healed; save me, and I shall be saved; for you are my praise." (Jeremiah 17:14)

DEC 13

Unable to heal myself, I notice and receive God's care.

"We do not know what to do, but our eyes are on you." (2 Chronicles 20:12)

Identifying The Voice to Trust

The voice that lies whispers that you are not worth loving
and that God cannot be trusted. But you know that this
is not God's voice. God's voice says, "I love you. I'm here.
I am the one who is with you and for you." This is the
voice Jesus knew intimately and trusted daily. Like Jesus,
you can depend on what God has spoken in the past, to
others and to you. God's voice resonates with the truth
of the Scriptures and always confirms what is most true
about you, about God, and about others. What is most
true is that God is love. God's truth has real traction to
set you free. As God's Spirit whispers truth to your deep
places, the opinions of others and the hiss of the deceiver
are silenced.

JAN 14

I listen for the voice that can be trusted.

"For your steadfast love is before my eyes, and I walk in faithfulness to you." (Psalm 26:3)

FEB 14

In every moment, God speaks truth.

"So shall my word be that goes out from my mouth; it shall not return to me empty, but it shall accomplish that which I purpose." (Isaiah 55:11)

MAR 14

The voice that speaks truth confirms that God is with me.

"Know that I am with you and will keep you wherever you go, and will bring you back to this land; for I will not leave you." (Genesis 28:15)

APR 14

Rejecting hollow words, I embrace what is solid.

"You must understand this, my beloved: let everyone be quick to listen, slow to speak, slow to anger." (James 1:19)

MAY 14

I trust the voice that says I belong to God.

"And a voice came from heaven, 'You are my Son, the Beloved; with you I am well pleased.'" (Luke 3:22)

JUN 14

The patient and kind One welcomes me to draw near.

"Listen! I am standing at the door, knocking; if you hear my voice and open the door, I will come in to you and eat with you, and you with me." (Revelation 3:20)

JUL 14

God's Spirit opens my heart to receive what is true.

"But the Advocate, the Holy Spirit, whom the Father will send in my name, will teach you everything, and remind you of all that I have said to you." (John 14:26)

AUG 14

I trust the voice that says, "I am with you and for you."

"When he has brought out all his own, he goes ahead of them, and the sheep follow him because they know his voice." (John 10:4)

SEP 14

As I choose what is most real, others' opinions have less weight.

"But Peter and the apostles answered, 'We must obey God rather than any human authority.'" (Acts 5:29)

OCT 14

I hear God most clearly through God's written word.

"All scripture is inspired by God and is useful for teaching, for re-proof, for correction, and for training in righteousness." (2 Timothy 3:16)

NOV 14

God has spoken in the past, and God speaks today.

"He said further, 'I am the God of your father, the God of Abraham, the God of Isaac, and the God of Jacob.'" (Exodus 3:6)

DEC 14

I hear and trust the voice that spoke at Jesus' baptism.

"A voice came from the cloud, saying, 'This is my Son, whom I have chosen; listen to him.'" (Luke 9:35)

Practicing Self-Care

You matter. Because you are created in God's image, nothing in this world or the next can change your inherent worth. In fact, Jesus' command to love others the way you love yourself *presumes* that you are worthy of loving care. Imitating God's own acceptance of you, you are choosing to embrace what is most true about you and about God. Caring for your heart, mind, body, and spirit, by treating yourself with loving-kindness, honors the one who made you and who loves you. Your posture of self-acceptance blesses you and blesses those around you; caring for yourself gives others permission to do the same. As you choose to live from the solid place, your daily choices confirm that you are worthy and precious to God. You are worthy of loving care.

JAN 15

Received by God, I am free to be who I really am.

"But by the grace of God I am what I am..." (1 Corinthians 15:10)

FEB 15

I treat myself with the loving-kindness I extend to others.

"As God's chosen ones, holy and beloved, clothe yourselves with compassion, kindness, humility, meekness, and patience." (Colossians 3:12)

MAR 15

I honor God by protecting my body, heart, and mind.

"O God, be merciful to me, for in you my soul takes refuge; in the shadow of your wings I will take refuge, until the destroying storms pass by." (Psalm 57:1)

APR 15

I accept myself the way God has accepted me.

"I tell you, this man went down to his home justified." (Luke 18:14)

MAY 15

I can be weak.

"My grace is sufficient for you, for power is made perfect in weakness." (2 Corinthians 12:9)

JUN 15

I receive the compassion Jesus has for those who suffer.

"When he went ashore, he saw a great crowd; and he had compassion for them and cured their sick." (Matthew 14:14)

JUL 15

Accepting myself as I am, I allow others to do the same.

"The second is this, 'You shall love your neighbor as yourself.' There is no other commandment greater than these." (Mark 12:31)

AUG 15

I have permission to be exactly where I am on the journey.

"And all of us, with unveiled faces, seeing the glory of the Lord as though reflected in a mirror, are being transformed into the same image." (2 Corinthians 3:18)

SEP 15

I honor God as I care for myself the way I care for others.

"You do well if you really fulfill the royal law according to the scripture, 'You shall love your neighbor as yourself.'" (James 2:8)

OCT 15

God does not love me more than or less than others.

"But God, who is rich in mercy, out of the great love with which he loved us…made us alive together with Christ." (Ephesians 2:4-5)

NOV 15

When I dare to reveal my real self, I invite God's healing.

"Therefore confess your sins to one another, and pray for one another, so that you may be healed. The prayer of the righteous is powerful and effective." (James 5:16)

DEC 15

When I humble myself, God receives me.

"But the tax collector, standing far off, would not even look up to heaven, but was beating his breast and saying, 'God, be merciful to me, a sinner!' I tell you this man went down to his home justified." (Luke 18:13-14)

Traveling With Faithful Companions

Some are not able or willing to be with you and for you in the ways you most want and need them to be. So you are choosing carefully those with whom you share your heart. Those who have faced their own suffering, and daily choose to live from the solid place, are often well equipped to journey with you. The faithful companion mirrors that you are worth loving and noticing. This one reflects who you really are. His or her ears listen patiently and without judgment. The lips of this faithful one announce what is most true about you, about others, and about God. He or she takes a real interest in your life and receives every part of you. The one committed to your wellbeing is God's good gift to you.

JAN 16

I give thanks for the faithful guides God has provided.

"For I brought you up from the land of Egypt, and redeemed you from the house of slavery; and I sent before you Moses, Aaron, and Miriam." (Micah 6:4)

FEB 16

My faithful companions pray with me and for me.

"First of all, then, I urge that supplications, prayers, intercessions, and thanksgivings be made for everyone." (1 Timothy 2:1)

MAR 16

I choose my friends wisely.

"Some friends play at friendship but a true friend sticks closer than one's nearest kin." (Proverbs 18:24)

APR 16

The face of the faithful companion reflects my worth.

"Then Jonathan made a covenant with David, because he loved him as his own soul." (1 Samuel 18:3)

MAY 16

I trust the one who proclaims God's truth as reality.

"I have called you friends, because I have made known to you everything that I have heard from my Father." (John 15:15)

JUN 16

A faithful companion reflects, for me, my true self.

"Therefore encourage one another and build up each other, as indeed you are doing." (1 Thessalonians 5:11)

JUL 16

The faithful friend takes a genuine interest in my life.

"Do not seek your own advantage, but that of the other." (1 Corinthians 10:24)

AUG 16

The faithful companion sees me and hears me.

"The hearing ear and the seeing eye—the Lord has made them both." (Proverbs 20:12)

SEP 16

I journey with those who are committed to my well-being.

"Iron sharpens iron, and one person sharpens the wits of another." (Proverbs 27:17)

OCT 16

The one who has known affliction comforts me.

"We may be able to console those who are in any affliction with the consolation with which we ourselves are consoled by God." (2 Corinthians 1:4)

NOV 16

A faithful friend sees in me what I can't yet see.

"Whoever walks with the wise becomes wise, but the companion of fools suffers harm." (Proverbs 13:20)

DEC 16

I choose to be vulnerable with those who can be trusted.

"A friend loves at all times, and kinsfolk are born to share adversity." (Proverbs 17:17)

Honoring Your Feelings

Your feelings are real, but they are not reality. Their job is to signal something that is worth noticing. Resisting your feelings gives them power. When you resist a feeling—sadness, anger, or fear—it will stay, whether it's silently buried in your deep places or pulsing palpably in your body. In the moments when you are undone, the deceiver hisses that your feelings will overwhelm you. Or he convinces you that you cannot bear to face them. But this is a lie. As you decide to allow your feelings, you are discovering that you are able to bear them and learn what they have to teach you. As you allow your feelings, and release them, you dispel their power to undo you.

JAN 17

I notice uncomfortable feelings, allowing them to pass.

"Be strong, and let your heart take courage, all you who wait for the Lord." (Psalm 31:24)

FEB 17

My feelings are real, but they are not reality.

"The heart is devious above all else; it is perverse—who can understand it?" (Jeremiah 17:9)

MAR 17

With Jesus' love in me, I need not fear being abandoned.

"Since God loved us so much, we also ought to love one another." (1 John 4:11)

APR 17

Because love conquers fear, I speak and live confidently.

"For if you keep silence at such a time as this, relief and deliverance will rise for the Jews from another quarter." (Esther 4:14)

MAY 17

I notice my sadness, allow it, and let it pass by.

"Jesus began to weep." (John 11:35)

JUN 17

As love gains traction, fear's grip is weakened.

"There is no fear in love, but perfect love casts out fear; for fear has to do with punishment, and whoever fears has not reached perfection in love." (1 John 4:18)

JUL 17

My feelings no longer cut me off from what's most real.

"…and free those who all their lives were held in slavery by the fear of death." (Hebrews 2:15)

AUG 17

Allowing feelings, not numbing them, is the way to life.

"The Lord is my light and my salvation; whom shall I fear? The Lord is the stronghold of my life; of whom shall I be afraid?" (Psalm 27:1)

SEP 17

I am not bullied by fear.

"They are not afraid of evil tidings; their hearts are firm, secure in the Lord." (Psalm 112:7)

OCT 17

I notice my anxiety and release it to the One who cares.

"Do not fear, for I am with you, do not be afraid, for I am your God; I will strengthen you, I will help you." (Isaiah 41:10)

NOV 17

I exercise courage as I notice and feel my feelings.

"For you did not receive a spirit of slavery to fall back into fear, but you have received a spirit of adoption. When we cry, 'Abba! Father!' it is that very Spirit bearing witness with our spirit that we are children of God." (Romans 8:15)

DEC 17

Like Jesus, I offer my anxious feelings to the Father.

"In his anguish he prayed more earnestly, and his sweat became like great drops of blood falling down on the ground." (Luke 22:44)

Connecting to God

The enemy's predictable strategy is to suggest that God is not available to you. But you are recognizing this devious voice as the voice that lies. Like Jesus, you refuse to agree because you know that God cares for you. You are aware that God is near. In any moment, you may not feel God's palpable presence or understand God's timing. This is natural. Yet you know that the Father of Jesus, who delivered the Israelites out of captivity in Egypt and liberated Jesus from the grave, can be trusted. Every time you agree that God is with you and for you, you live from the solid place. In this moment, and all others, God is available to you.

JAN 18

In every moment God's voice whispers: "I am for you."

"If God is for us, who is against us?" (Romans 8:31)

FEB 18

I begin the rest of my journey with God from where I am right now.

"The Lord is near to all who call on him." (Psalm 145:18)

MAR 18

I turn my face toward the One who is gracious.

"Return to the Lord, your God, for he is gracious and merciful, slow to anger, and abounding in steadfast love, and relents from punishing." (Joel 2:13)

APR 18

My relationship with God need not look like another's.

"O Lord, you have searched me and known me." (Psalm 139:1)

MAY 18

I encounter God in typical and in unlikely circumstances.

"The Lord is good to those who wait for him, to the soul that seeks him." (Lamentations 3:25)

JUN 18

I choose to abide in God, my truest home.

"At that time I will bring you home, at the time when I gather you." (Zephaniah 3:20)

JUL 18

In this moment and all others, God is with me and for me.

"Where can I go from your spirit? Or where can I flee from your presence?" (Psalm 139:7)

AUG 18

I may not understand God's timing, but I trust God.

"The Lord is not slow about his promise, as some think of slowness, but is patient with you, not wanting any to perish, but all to come to repentance." (2 Peter 3:9)

SEP 18

God offers me what I most need.

"And my God will fully satisfy every need of yours according to his riches in glory in Christ Jesus." (Philippians 4:19)

OCT 18

My journey with God is entirely, uniquely my own.

"In all your ways acknowledge him, and he will make straight your paths." (Proverbs 3:6)

NOV 18

My ugly parts cannot dissuade God from loving me.

"Though your sins are like scarlet, they shall be like snow; though they are red like crimson, they shall become like wool." (Isaiah 1:18)

DEC 18

God empowered Jesus, and God empowers me.

"God anointed Jesus of Nazareth with the Holy Spirit and with power" (Acts 10:38)

Receiving God's Provision

Exploiting your past, a lying voice took up residence in your deep places and insisted that you were not enough and you were not forgiven. You are choosing to reject what is false and embrace what is most true about God's unfailing grace for you. You are receiving this life-giving reality through the Scriptures, through God's Spirit in prayer, through faithful companions, and through helping professionals God provides. God's truth, love, and forgiveness are being expressed through human faces and voices. As you accept the truth they offer, you receive God's own care for you. Embracing the immutability of your belovedness, you choose for the solid place.

JAN 19

Gracious human faces reflect God's steadfast love.

"Where you die, I will die—there will I be buried. May the Lord do thus and so to me, and more as well, if even death parts me from you!" (Ruth 1:17)

FEB 19

I receive God's unfailing forgiveness.

"For the Lord your God is gracious and merciful, and will not turn away his face from you, if you return to him." (2 Chronicles 30:9)

MAR 19

I receive God's care through those who love me.

"For where two or three are gathered in my name, I am there among them. (Matthew 18:20)

APR 19

I recognize the sound of God's voice and I respond to it.

"My sheep hear my voice. I know them, and they follow me." (John 10:27)

MAY 19

I receive care from helping professionals as God's own care.

"Now there are varieties of gifts, but the same Spirit." (1 Corinthians 12:4)

JUN 19

Exactly as I am, I accept Jesus' welcome and forgiveness.

"I have come to call not the righteous but sinners to repentance." (Luke 5:32)

JUL 19

I receive the robust nourishment God offers.

"Ask, and it will be given you; search, and you will find." (Matthew 7:7)

AUG 19

I receive the care of those who are with me and for me.

"For though I am absent in body, yet I am with you in spirit..." (Colossians 2:5)

SEP 19

I receive with gratitude the good gifts offered to me by others.

"Serve one another with whatever gift each of you has received." (1 Peter 4:10)

OCT 19

Identified by Christ's blood, I am a child of God.

"But to all who received him, who believed in his name, he gave power to become children of God, who were born, not of blood or of the will of the flesh or of the will of man, but of God." (John 1:12-13)

NOV 19

I wait patiently for God's provision.

"Yet the LORD longs to be gracious to you; therefore he will rise up to show you compassion ... Blessed are all who wait for him!" (Isaiah 30:18)

DEC 19

I give and receive God's own love.

"You yourselves have been taught by God to love one another." (1 Thessalonians 4:9)

Claiming Your Belovedness

Though you've been willing to believe that God loves others, it has been more difficult to receive God's unfailing love for you in your deep places. Your fleeting sadness, anger, and fear feel more palpable than the concrete fact of your belovedness. In every moment, past, present, and future, you have been, are, and will be held in God's love. Daily you are choosing for this unchanging reality. You can see a face of love that shines upon you. You can hear God's voice affirming, "You belong to me. Nothing can change my love for you." You are discovering that the substance of your belovedness is more solid and sure than anything that tries to threaten it. Now and forever, you are God's beloved.

JAN 20

In this moment, I am loved.

"Steadfast love surrounds those who trust in the Lord." (Psalm 32:10)

FEB 20

Nothing can change my inherent belovedness.

"In this is love, not that we loved God but that he loved us and sent his Son to be the atoning sacrifice for our sins." (1 John 4:10)

MAR 20

God's constant whisper affirms, "You are mine."

"Do not fear, for I have redeemed you; I have called you by name, you are mine." (Isaiah 43:1)

APR 20

Nothing can keep me from God's love.

"Who can hide in secret places so that I cannot see them? says the Lord. Do I not fill heaven and earth? says the Lord." (Jeremiah 23:24)

MAY 20

Now and forever, I am loved beyond measure.

"I have loved you with an everlasting love; therefore I have continued my faithfulness to you." (Jeremiah 31:3)

JUN 20

Because Christ lives in me, I receive God's unfailing love.

"It is no longer I who live, but it is Christ who lives in me." (Galatians 2:20)

JUL 20

What is most real and most true is that I am loved.

"He will rejoice over you with gladness, he will renew you in his love; he will exult over you with loud singing." (Zephaniah 3:17)

AUG 20

Past, present, and future, I am beloved.

"But the steadfast love of the Lord is from everlasting to everlasting on those who fear him, and his righteousness to children's children." (Psalm 103:17)

SEP 20

I am not defined by what I do, but by whose I am.

"If we live, we live to the Lord, and if we die, we die to the Lord; so then, whether we live or whether we die, we are the Lord's." (Romans 14:8)

OCT 20

The choices of others cannot change my belovedness.

"Beloved, we are God's children now." (1 John 3:2)

NOV 20

I am loved.

"For I am convinced that neither death, nor life...nor anything else in all creation, will be able to separate us from the love of God in Christ Jesus our Lord." (Romans 8:38-39)

DEC 20

I belong to God, and nothing can change that.

"But you are a chosen race, a royal priesthood, a holy nation, God's own people." (1 Peter 2:9)

Entrusting Others to God

You suffer when you wish those around you to be other than they are. But as you learn to accept others, as they are and not as they should be, you experience palpable relief. This liberating choice is available to you in each moment. When you notice a niggling destructive thought—"It's his fault I'm suffering," "What she did is unforgivable," or "He's to blame"—you choose life as you consciously release the offender, real or imagined. This is not an endorsement of the other's behavior; it is a decision to trust God with what is. As you lovingly release individuals who have not cared for you in the past, or are ill-equipped to care for you now, you choose to live from the solid place.

JAN 21

When I want to blame, I release the person to God.

"Why do you see the speck in your neighbor's eye, but do not notice the log in your own eye?" (Matthew 7:3)

FEB 21

I forgive those who have not loved me well.

"At my first defense no one came to my support, but all deserted me. May it not be counted against them!" (2 Timothy 4:16)

MAR 21

I extend loving-kindness to those unable to support me.

"But I say to you, Love your enemies and pray for those who persecute you." (Matthew 5:44)

APR 21

Those who ignore my suffering fail to embody God's care.

"The tongue of the wise dispenses knowledge, but the mouths of fools pour out folly." (Proverbs 15:2)

MAY 21

I shift my gaze from the faces of others to the face of God.

"Seek the Lord and his strength, seek his presence continually." (1 Chronicles 16:11)

JUN 21

I release those who've not cared for themselves or for me.

"The righteous gives good advice to friends, but the way of the wicked leads astray." (Proverbs 12:26)

JUL 21

Those who failed me do not define me.

"Do not fret because of the wicked; do not be envious of wrongdoers." (Psalm 37:1)

AUG 21

I don't seek love from those unable to receive me.

"Or am I trying to please people? If I were still pleasing people, I would not be a servant of Christ." (Galatians 1:10)

SEP 21

When others fail to care for me, I graciously release them.

"He has put my family far from me, and my acquaintances are wholly estranged from me." (Job 9:13)

OCT 21

I release my desire to receive what others can't give.

"Do not put your trust in princes, in mortals, in whom there is no help." (Psalm 146:3)

NOV 21

I honor God by releasing those who are unsafe.

"You will know them by their fruits. Are grapes gathered from thorns, or figs from thistles?" (Matthew 7:16)

DEC 21

I release those who do not receive me.

"It is better to take refuge in the Lord than to put confidence in mortals." (Psalm 118:8)

Trusting A Faithful Parent

The faces and voices of your earliest caregivers, both those who were present and those who were absent, prefigured what you expected of a divine other. This is natural. Yet every parent, in varying degrees, will fail. In God's face, you receive the exuberant and unconditional welcome you did not receive from human faces. You hear a voice that is calm, gracious, and kind. You taste what's available to you now: perfect steadfast love for which you were made. You are being transformed as reality penetrates your deep places. As a loving mother holds and nurtures her child, God is with you. As a good father protects and empowers his child, God is for you. What you most need is available to you now. God is the faithful parent who does not fail.

JAN 22

Like a loving mother, God catches me when I fall.

"As an eagle stirs up its nest, and hovers over its young; as it spreads its wings, takes them up, and bears them aloft on its pinions." *(Deuteronomy 32:11)*

FEB 22

Jesus reveals the love of the Father.

"Jesus said to him, 'Have I been with you all this time, Philip, and you still do not know me? Whoever has seen me has seen the Father.'" *(John 14:9)*

MAR 22

In every moment a reliable parent is with me and for me.

"If my father and mother forsake me, the Lord will take me up." *(Psalm 27:10)*

APR 22

My heavenly Father, not my earthly one, defines me.

*"And call no one your father on earth, for you have one Father—
the one in heaven." (Matthew 23:9)*

MAY 22

God comforts me as a loving mother consoles her
child.

*"As a mother comforts her child, so I will comfort you; you shall be
comforted in Jerusalem." (Isaiah 66:13)*

JUN 22

God, the Father, has listened through God, the Son.

*"He had to become like his brothers and sisters in every respect, so
that he might be a merciful and faithful high priest in the service
of God" (Hebrews 2:17)*

JUL 22

God is a parent who gives good gifts.

"If you then, who are evil, know how to give good gifts to your children, how much more will your Father in heaven give good things." (Matthew 7:11)

AUG 22

On the cross, the Father gave his own life for me.

"The Father and I are one." (John 10:30)

SEP 22

I hear God speak clearly through the Son.

"Long ago God spoke to our ancestors in many and various ways by the prophets, but in these last days he has spoken to us by a Son." (Hebrews 1:1-2)

OCT 22

God cares for me like a nurturing mother.

"I led them with cords of human kindness, with bands of love. I was to them like those who lift infants to their cheeks. I bent down to them and fed them." (Hosea 11:4)

NOV 22

Today a father who is good receives me in love.

"See what love the Father has given us, that we should be called children of God; and that is what we are." (1 John 3:1)

DEC 22

God is the loving parent I have always needed.

"Can a woman forget her nursing child, or show no compassion for the child of her womb? Even these may forget, yet I will not forget you." (Isaiah 49:15)

Rejecting The Voice That Lies

Vying for your attention and allegiance, the voice that lies distorts what is true about God, about you, and about others. This is the voice that tempted Eve in the garden and Jesus in the wilderness, warping reality by twisting what is true. Yet Jesus rejected the devil's lie by trusting in God's love and faithfulness. With the Father's voice still echoing in his heart and mind from his baptism—"This is my Son, the beloved, with whom I am well pleased" (Matthew 3:17)—Jesus refused the deceiver's crooked logic. In each moment, the Spirit is helping you to recognize, trust, and obey the voice that Jesus trusted. In rejecting the voice that lies, you live from the solid place.

JAN 23

I reject the voice that tells me I am not enough.

"When he lies, he speaks according to his own nature, for he is a liar and the father of lies." (John 8:44)

FEB 23

I reject the voice that twists the truth.

"Even Satan disguises himself as an angel of light." (2 Corinthians 11:14)

MAR 23

I reject the voice that says I deserved what I've endured.

"Put on the whole armor of God, so that you may be able to stand against the wiles of the devil." (Ephesians 6:11)

APR 23

I reject the voice insisting I'm defined by my past.

"Do not remember the sins of my youth or my transgressions; according to your steadfast love remember me, for your goodness' sake, O Lord!" (Psalm 25:7)

MAY 23

I reject the voice hissing that God is not for me.

"Now the serpent was more crafty than any other wild animal that the Lord God had made. He said to the woman, 'Did God say...?'" (Genesis 3:1)

JUN 23

I reject the voice that says that my faith is not enough.

"For it is the Gentiles who strive for all these things; and indeed your heavenly Father knows that you need all these things." (Matthew 6:32)

JUL 23

I reject the voice insisting that others' actions define me.

"By this I know that you are pleased with me; because my enemy has not triumphed over me." (Psalm 41:11)

AUG 23

I reject the voice contending that I do not know God.

"I am the good shepherd. I know my own and my own know me." (John 10:14)

SEP 23

I reject the voice insisting I will never find relief.

"He will wipe every tear from their eyes. Death will be no more; mourning and crying and pain will be no more." (Revelation 21:4)

OCT 23

I reject the voice whispering that I am not loved by God.

"For as the heavens are high above the earth, so great is his stead-fast love toward those who fear him." (Psalm 103:11)

NOV 23

I reject the voice attacking me with guilt and shame.

"Your adversary the devil prowls around like a roaring lion, seeking someone to devour." (1 Peter 5:8)

DEC 23

I reject the voice telling me I am not loved by others.

"Beloved, let us love one another, because love is from God; everyone who loves is born of God and knows God." (1 John 4:7)

Welcoming God's Healing

Wounds that remain in the dark will continue to throb. But you are allowing your old hurts to surface, exposing them to light and air and truth. As you do, you are being healed. When you feel the sting of a wound you've faced before, one that you assumed had been healed or forgiven, resist the impulse to shame yourself. This is an opportunity to explore the new depths or fresh nuances of healing. While the process may be uncomfortable, and may not unfold according to your schedule, you have confidence in God's faithfulness. As sin is forgiven and shame is debunked, God is redeeming all you have endured. God is the one who heals and forgives.

JAN 24

God is healing my broken heart.

"...he has sent me to bring good news to the oppressed, to bind up the brokenhearted..." (Isaiah 61:1)

FEB 24

I welcome trusted friends to share my journey of healing.

"Are any among you sick? They should call for the elders of the church and have them pray over them..." (James 5:14)

MAR 24

There is opportunity, not shame, in old pain resurfacing.

"For freedom Christ has set us free. Stand firm, therefore, and do not submit again to a yoke of slavery." (Galatians 5:1)

APR 24

Wounds heal when they're exposed to light and air.

"For once you were darkness, but now in the Lord you are light. Live as children of light." (Ephesians 5:8)

MAY 24

Jesus may heal me gradually.

"Then Jesus laid his hands on his eyes again; and he looked intently and his sight was restored, and he saw everything clearly." (Mark 8:25)

JUN 24

When an old wound ruptures, I offer it for healing.

"Great crowds came to him, bringing with them the lame, the maimed, the blind, the mute, and many others." (Matthew 15:30)

JUL 24

Noticing and facing my pain is the unlikely way to healing.

"Those who go out weeping, bearing the seed for sowing, shall come home with shouts of joy, carrying their sheaves." (Psalm 126:6)

AUG 24

The wounds I am willing to face can be healed.

"I have heard your prayer, I have seen your tears; indeed, I will heal you." (2 Kings 20:5)

SEP 24

When buried pain resurfaces, I offer it to God.

"He heals the brokenhearted, and binds up their wounds." (Psalm 147:3)

OCT 24

God redeems what I have endured.

"Therefore I am content with weaknesses, insults, hardships, persecutions, and calamities for the sake of Christ; for whenever I am weak, then I am strong." (2 Corinthians 12:10)

NOV 24

The pace of my healing is in God's hands.

"For my thoughts are not your thoughts, nor are your ways my ways, says the Lord." (Isaiah 55:8)

DEC 24

God forgives all my sin.

"But if we walk in the light as he himself is in the light, we have fellowship with one another, and the blood of Jesus his Son cleanses us from all sin." (1 John 1:7)

Knowing Jesus

Since your earliest days, you have longed for a face that does not go away. Jesus—the one who disappeared for a moment and returned on the third day—has become the steadfast, faithful countenance that does not fail. Having faced the powers of sin and death, Jesus knows what your life is like. Nothing you have endured was not borne by Jesus on the cross. Jesus sees you. Jesus hears you. Jesus knows you. Jesus loves you. Jesus prays for you. The good news is this: in Jesus, the Father has given his own life out of love for you. You live from the solid place as you agree that Jesus is present to you now. In every moment, the voice of Jesus whispers, "I am the One who is with you and for you."

JAN 25

Jesus notices me.

"Some were saying, 'It is he.' Others were saying, 'No, but it is someone like him.' He kept saying, 'I am the man.'" (John 9:9)

FEB 25

God's anointed one understands my suffering.

"He was despised and rejected by others; a man of suffering and acquainted with infirmity; and as one from whom others hide their faces." (Isaiah 53:3)

MAR 25

Jesus prays for me.

"Consequently he is able for all time to save those who approach God through him, since he always lives to make intercession for them." (Hebrews 7:25)

APR 25

There is no evil, pain, sin, or burden Christ did not bear.

"Surely he has borne our infirmities and carried our diseases; yet we accounted him stricken, struck down by God, and afflicted." (Isaiah 53:4)

MAY 25

God tasted death to free me from the one who wields it.

"He himself likewise shared the same things, so that through death he might destroy the one who has the power of death, that is, the devil." (Hebrews 2:14)

JUN 25

Jesus accompanies me.

"Abide in me as I abide in you." (John 15:4)

JUL 25

Jesus intercedes for me.

"Who is to condemn? It is Christ Jesus, who died, yes, who was raised, who is at the right hand of God, who indeed intercedes for us." (Romans 8:34)

AUG 25

Jesus is with me on the journey.

"For where two or three are gathered in my name, I am there among them." (Matthew 18:20)

SEP 25

The one who took on flesh knows what my life is like.

"For we do not have a high priest who is unable to sympathize with our weaknesses, but we have one who in every respect has been tested as we are..." (Hebrews 4:15)

OCT 25

Jesus is able to help me.

"Because he himself was tested by what he suffered, he is able to help those who are being tested." (Hebrews 2:18)

NOV 25

Jesus loves me with the same love the Father has for him.

"As the Father has loved me, so I have loved you; abide in my love." (John 15:9)

DEC 25

Jesus came to be with me and for me.

"And the Word became flesh and lived among us, and we have seen his glory, the glory as of a father's only son, full of grace and truth." (John 1:14)

Extending and Receiving Forgiveness

You long to be free. And yet in those places where you
have not forgiven others, or have not received God's
gracious mercy, you remain stuck. You rehearse blame.
You feel unworthy. Beloved, your fear that forgiving will
condone the wrongs of others is natural. So is your fear
that the forgiveness extended to you—divine or human—
will not be effective. Yet as you choose to release the sins
God has forgiven, both yours and others', you are being
set free. You will not, and need not, forget the wrongs
done to you, or those you have committed, but they will
no longer exercise power over you. As you give and receive
forgiveness, you are being set free.

JAN 26

I am forgiven by the gracious one.

"To the Lord our God belong mercy and forgiveness, for we have rebelled against him." (Daniel 9:9)

FEB 26

I choose life as I release wrongs committed against me.

"Let anyone among you who is without sin be the first to throw a stone at her." (John 8:7)

MAR 26

If those who hurt me never confess, I can still be free.

"For if you forgive others their trespasses, your heavenly Father will also forgive you." (Matthew 6:14)

APR 26

I choose to practice forgiveness.

"'How often should I forgive? As many as seven times?' Jesus said to him, 'Not seven times, but, I tell you, seventy-seven times.'" (Matthew 18:21-22)

MAY 26

Unforgiveness keeps me bound; forgiveness sets me free.

"Do not judge, and you will not be judged; do not condemn, and you will not be condemned. Forgive, and you will be forgiven." (Luke 6:37)

JUN 26

Where relationships are still broken, I choose forgiveness.

"Whenever you stand praying, forgive, if you have anything against anyone; so that your Father in heaven may also forgive you your trespasses." (Mark 11:25)

JUL 26

I forgive and release sins God has forgiven and released.

*"As far as the east is from the west, so far he removes our transgres-
sions from us." (Psalm 103:12)*

AUG 26

I can notice the wrongs done to me, even as I let them
go.

*"Wait for the Lord; be strong, and let your heart take courage."
(Psalm 27:14)*

SEP 26

I don't forget the past, but I'm no longer bound by it.

*"Bear with one another and, if anyone has a complaint against an-
other, forgive each other; just as the Lord has forgiven you, so you
also must forgive." (Colossians 3:13)*

OCT 26

I choose freedom when I refuse to rehearse blame.

"Love ... is not ... resentful." (1 Corinthians 13:4-5)

NOV 26

I outwit the enemy when I choose to forgive.

"And we do this so that we may not be outwitted by Satan; for we are not ignorant of his designs." (2 Corinthians 2:11)

DEC 26

I seek forgiveness from those I have hurt or offended.

"So when you are offering your gift at the altar, if you remember that your brother or sister has something against you." (Matthew 5:23)

Facing your Longings and Temptations

You long to be seen, heard, known, and loved. Of course. And you naturally prefer comfort over distress. This is why, when you've felt undone, you've been tempted to turn to soothing substitutes—comforts, habits, people— that do not truly satisfy. But you know that the deepest needs of your heart are most fully satisfied by the one whose love does not fail. So you are learning to receive what God provides by releasing your longings and temptations to the One who can be trusted. When you notice you are sinking, by turning to counterfeit comforts, you can self-correct and return to the solid place. Refusing what does not satisfy, you choose to tolerate discomfort by making small choices for life that truly is life. Because Christ lives in you, you can bear what is.

JAN 27

I hear and respond to the voice I trust.

"The gatekeeper opens the gate for him, and the sheep hear his voice. He calls his own sheep by name and leads them out." (John 10:3)

FEB 27

My deep longing to be seen and known is being met by God.

"Many Samaritans from that city believed in him because of the woman's testimony, 'He told me everything I have ever done.'" (John 4:39)

MAR 27

Resisting the temptation to hide, I can be who I truly am.

"The man and his wife hid themselves from…the Lord God…" (Genesis 3:8)

APR 27

The accepting gaze I've longed for is available in Jesus.

"When Jesus came to the place, he looked up and said to him, 'Zacchaeus, hurry and come down; for I must stay at your house today.'" (Luke 19:5)

MAY 27

I will not force or avoid my natural longing for intimacy.

"My frame was not hidden from you, when I was being made in secret, intricately woven in the depths of the earth." (Psalm 139:15)

JUN 27

Refusing to engineer my own redemption, I wait on God.

"God is faithful, and he will not let you be tested beyond your strength, but with the testing he will also provide the way out." (1 Corinthians 10:13)

JUL 27

When tempted to trust the wrong people, I turn to God.

"And to the man he said, 'Because you have listened to the voice of your wife … cursed is the ground because of you.'" (Genesis 3:17)

AUG 27

God satisfies my natural longing to be known and loved.

"I have observed the misery of my people … I have heard their cry…Indeed, I know their sufferings, and I have come down to deliver them…'" (Exodus 3:7-8)

SEP 27

I refuse to offer to others what I've not offered to God.

"O people; pour out your heart before him; God is a refuge for us." (Psalm 62:8)

OCT 27

God knows, intimately, the aches of my heart.

"O Lord, all my longing is known to you; my sighing is not hidden from you." (Psalm 38:9)

NOV 27

I refuse to allow another person to determine my worth.

"They answered him, 'Abraham is our father.' Jesus said to them, 'If you were Abraham's children, you would be doing what Abraham did.'" (John 8:39)

DEC 27

Tempted by that which doesn't satisfy, I turn to Jesus.

"Come to me, all you that are weary and are carrying heavy burdens, and I will give you rest." (Matthew 11:28)

Caring for Others

In the past, old hurts interfered with your relationships, both human and divine. But as you are being made well, you are being equipped to give and receive love freely. Having faced your own suffering, you are able to be present to others because you can now allow and bear what is. Grounded in the reality of God's love, you are able to be with and for others. You are even being released to forgive and accept those who've hurt you, as you exercise wisdom, kindness, and healthy boundaries. Rooted in what is most real, you reflect God's own steadfast, loving presence to others. You are fully equipped to do what you were made to do: give and receive love, both human and divine. So you love others the way Jesus loves you.

JAN 28

As I heal, I'm free to move toward those who suffer.

"We must support the weak, remembering the words of the Lord Jesus, for he himself said, 'It is more blessed to give than to receive.'" (Acts 20:35)

FEB 28

With wisdom, I can love the person who hurt me.

"But love your enemies, do good, and lend, expecting nothing in return. Your reward will be great, and you will be children of the Most High." (Luke 6:35)

MAR 28

I am growing in my capacity to give and receive love.

"You shall love your neighbor as yourself." (Matthew 22:39)

APR 28

As God refreshes me, I'm able to receive ones who are weary.

"Bear one another's burdens, and in this way you will fulfill the law of Christ." (Galatians 6:2)

MAY 28

I can choose to be the friend I wish had befriended me.

"Do to others as you would have them do to you." (Luke 6:31)

JUN 28

My heart is being made tender toward those who suffer.

"Many are the afflictions of the righteous, but the Lord rescues them from them all." (Psalm 34:19)

JUL 28

By accepting my own belovedness, I can best love others.

"Those who were not my people I will call 'my people,' and her who was not beloved I will call 'beloved.'" (Romans 9:25)

AUG 28

I can share the gifts I've received on my journey.

"To each is given the manifestation of the Spirit for the common good." (1 Corinthians 12:7)

SEP 28

By moving toward others who suffer, I imitate Jesus.

"He was wounded for our transgressions, crushed for our iniquities; upon him was the punishment that made us whole, and by his bruises we are healed." (Isaiah 53:5)

OCT 28

I reflect God's face and speak God's truth to others.

"But speaking the truth in love, we must grow up in every way into him who is the head, into Christ." (Ephesians 4:15)

NOV 28

Because God is with and for me, I am with and for others.

"By this everyone will know that you are my disciples, if you have love for one another." (John 13:35)

DEC 28

Love—for God, for myself, for others—is actionable.

"Little children, let us love, not in word or speech, but in truth and action." (1 John 3:18)

Carrying Tools for the Journey

When you were sinking, you were bullied by your thoughts, your feelings, and the voice that lies. But you are being equipped with all you need to live from the solid place. Daily you are choosing to access the tools God provides. You are embracing the radical acceptance you received at your baptism. You are being fed by God at Christ's table. You are being nourished by God's word. You are meeting God in prayer. You are being strengthened by fellowship with others. You reject all forms of lies, speaking aloud only what is true. Firmly grounded, your choices—your "yeses" and your "noes"—honor you, honor God, and honor others. Confident that the one who is good is with you on the journey, you have access to all you need to travel well.

JAN 29

My deepest hunger is met at the Lord's table.

"When he had given thanks, he broke it and said, 'This is my body that is for you. Do this in remembrance of me.'" (1 Corinthians 11:24)

FEB 29

God empowers me to say a healthy *no*.

"For the grace of God has appeared, bringing salvation to all, training us to renounce impiety and worldly passions, and in the present age to live lives that are self-controlled, upright, and godly." (Titus 2:11-12)

MAR 29

As I choose truth, the grip of sin and death weakens.

"God chose you as the first fruits for salvation through sanctification by the Spirit and through belief in the truth." (2 Thessalonians 2:13)

APR 29

God is nourishing me with all I need.

"While they were eating, he took a loaf of bread, and after blessing it he broke it, gave it to them, and said, 'Take; this is my body.'" *(Mark 14:22)*

MAY 29

A gracious Mother received me in my baptism.

"I will sprinkle clean water upon you, and you shall be clean from all your uncleannesses, and from all your idols I will cleanse you." *(Ezekiel 36:25)*

JUN 29

Through Scripture, I can know God.

"Indeed, the word of God is living and active, sharper than any two-edged sword, piercing until it divides soul from spirit, joints from marrow." (Hebrews 4:12)

JUL 29

When it's right, I speak a good, bold *yes*.

"Death and life are in the power of the tongue, and those who love it will eat its fruits." (Proverbs 18:21)

AUG 29

At the Lord's table, a faithful Father provides for me.

"While they were eating, Jesus took a loaf of bread, and after blessing it he broke it, gave it to the disciples, and said, 'Take, eat; this is my body.'" (Matthew 26:26)

SEP 29

I make space in my life for God to speak and move.

"So we fasted and petitioned our God for this, and he listened to our entreaty." (Ezra 8:23)

OCT 29

As it was with Jesus, the Psalms assure me of God's fidelity.

"Into your hand I commit my spirit; you have redeemed me, O Lord, faithful God." (Psalm 31:5)

NOV 29

Prayer primes me to notice what God is up to.

"Devote yourselves to prayer, keeping alert in it with thanksgiving." (Colossians 4:20)

DEC 29

In my baptism, I was accepted, once and for all.

"He saved us ... according to his mercy, through the water of rebirth and renewal by the Holy Spirit." (Titus 3:5)

Relating to Others

Though you know that human love does not fully satisfy, you are naturally tempted to turn to human faces to satisfy the deep needs of your heart. While some will reflect God's gracious loving-kindness, others are ill-equipped to receive you. To the degree that you wish these to be other than they are, you will experience frustration. So you are lovingly releasing them to God. As God heals your heart, offering steadfast love and faithfulness, your relationships may shift. This is natural. Aware that others are no better and no worse than you, you offer them the grace that God has shown you. Imitating Jesus, you accept others as they are and not as they should be. As you grow emotionally and spiritually, as you become emotionally healthy, you are more fully equipped to relate well to others.

JAN 30

Human love fails, but there is one whose love never fails.

"O give thanks to the God of heaven, for his steadfast love endures forever." (Psalm 136:26)

MAR 30

As I receive God's love, I'm equipped to love others.

"...let us love one another." (2 John 1:5)

APR 30

As my security in God grows, my relationships mature.

"So we have known and believe the love that God has for us. God is love and those who abide in love abide in God, and God abides in them." (1 John 4:16)

MAY 30

Others are as vulnerable and as precious as I am.

"For he knows how we were made; he remembers that we are dust." (Psalm 103:14-15)

JUN 30

I offer others the mercy and patience God extends to me.

"The Lord is merciful and gracious, slow to anger and abounding in steadfast love." (Psalm 103:8)

JUL 30

I am no better or worse than others.

"In everything do to others as you would have them do to you; for this is the law and the prophets." (Matthew 7:12)

AUG 30

I love others as I have been loved.

"This is my commandment, that you love one another as I have loved you." (John 15:12)

SEP 30

I choose to view others the way God sees them.

"Do not judge by appearances, but judge with right judgment."(-John 7:24)

OCT 30

I accept others as they are and not as they should be.

"Welcome one another, therefore, just as Christ has welcomed you, for the glory of God." (Romans 15:7)

NOV 30

I celebrate and am grateful for those who love me
well.

*"Many proclaim themselves loyal, but who can find one worthy of
trust?" (Proverbs 20:6)*

DEC 30

My suffering has equipped me to love well.

*"Suffering produces endurance, and endurance produces character,
and character produces hope." (Romans 5:3-4)*

Exercising Gratitude

In the midst of circumstances you would not have chosen, gratitude may have once seemed incongruous with your experience. But you now recognize that embracing a posture of gratitude is life-giving, for you and for others. So you are giving thanks for the ways you've been delivered from the sting of sin and death. You are grateful for those who have embodied the reality of God's steadfast, faithful presence. Eyes open, you are able to notice the ways God has been with you and for you—on this day and throughout your lifetime. Today you are able to trust God for the future. As you live from the solid place, by choosing to exercise gratitude, you are being made well and set free.

JAN 31

I give thanks that God's love is stronger than death.

"He sent out his word and healed them, and delivered them from destruction." (Psalm 107:20)

MAR 31

I notice, and own, what God has already done for me.

"Did I not bring Israel up from the land of Egypt, and the Philistines from Caphtor and the Arameans from Kir?" (Amos 9:7)

MAY 31

I choose to practice gratitude by giving thanks today.

"Of course, there is great gain in godliness combined with contentment." (1 Timothy 6:6)

JUL 31

I give thanks for the faithful companions God provides.

"When David had finished speaking to Saul, the soul of Jonathan was bound to the soul of David, and Jonathan loved him as his own soul." (1 Samuel 18:1)

AUG 31

I give thanks that God is nourishing me.

"It is he ... who gives food to all flesh, for his steadfast love endures forever." (Psalm 136:13, 25)

OCT 31

I give thanks for God's love that does not fail.

"O give thanks to the Lord, for he is good; for his steadfast love endures forever." (1 Chronicles 16:34)

DEC 31

I notice the healing I've received, and I thank God.

"O give thanks to the Lord, for he is good; for his steadfast love endures forever." (Psalm 107:1)

My Story, Your Story, The Story

Margot Starbuck

"You are worthless garbage to be discarded."

Relinquished as an infant, adopted into a home impacted by violence, alcoholism, and divorce, I donned a girl-size suit of armor for emotional protection. Yet as I moved into adulthood and faced adult-sized challenges—accompanying a single friend through an unplanned pregnancy, being reunited with my birth mother, discovering and being rejected by my birth father, marrying in my mid-twenties—my ill-fitting girl-sized armor began to pinch and chafe. Without my permission, the pain and sadness I'd buried away in my deep places bubbled up through the unwelcome ruptures in my shell. The defenses that had served me well in childhood failed, and I came undone.

Exposed, I heard the sinister hiss of the enemy badgering, "*Of course* you're not worth showing up for or sticking around for. *Of course* you're not worth loving." On my bleakest days, that lying voice sounded more sensible than the voice that speaks truth.

As a person of faith, I yearned for the kind of healing transaction in which God would zap me well in an instant. However, my journey toward wholeness, stretching over a decade, was more lengthy and unwieldy than I would have chosen.

In my grief and confusion, God met me.

I began to hear God's gentle voice whispering, "I am for you." I recognized the words as those I'd most longed to hear from human lips. I had never seen them in the pages of Scripture before, yet suddenly they were emblazoned across each and every one. As I continued to listen, God confirmed and clarified, "I am the One who is with you and for you."

Clinging to this promise, I chose daily to agree that I was worth loving. That God's love was more real than my human experience of being forsaken. I was blessed to have the support of friends, family, wise professional guides, and the medication my body needed. Gradually, the voice that lies was silenced. My relationships—with my husband, with friends, with family—were transformed as the lies that had plagued me were replaced by what is most true.

Then, after eighteen years of marriage, my husband left me.

Seizing the opportunity, the voice that lies spoke up and hissed, "What about now? Are you worth loving *now*?"

God said *yes*.

Loved ones I trusted agreed with God.

But a loud abrasive voice continued to bully, "You are worthless garbage to be discarded."

In that painful season the One who does not lie reminded me, once again, that I was worthy. That I was beloved, by God and by others. That I didn't need to live as a victim of circumstance. That I was equipped to give and receive love. That I had all the resources I needed to flourish.

I was vivified by God's reliable presence when I needed it most.

The well-being I enjoy today—even when all is not as I would choose it to be—is why I've become convinced that you and I have all we need to thrive, emotionally and spiritually, when we choose to live from the solid place.

We see what it looks like to live from the solid place in the person of Jesus. Baptized in the Jordan, he is identified as God's beloved. Tempted in the wilderness, he rejects the deceiver's lies. Teetering at the edge of death, He trusts his Father for good, even in the midst of suffering.

Though your experience is unique, the One who is faithful knows all you've endured. Disappointment. Abandonment. Abuse. Loss. Loneliness. Addiction. Anxiety. Depression. Disease.

Whatever the circumstance, God whispers, to me and to you, "I am the One who is with you and for you."

Today you can choose to live from the solid place.

About the Author

Margot Starbuck is convinced that because God has chosen to be with us and for us—in the person of Jesus—we're made to be with and for others.

Margot is the author of over a dozen books. Her memoir, *The Girl in the Orange Dress: Searching for a Father Who Does Not Fail*, is about finding her birthparents as a young adult, coming undone, and being loved back together by the one who assured her, "I am for you." It was named the *2011 Nonfiction Book of the Year* by the Advanced Writers and Speakers Association.

Margot lives in Durham, North Carolina, with her three kiddos. Connect at www.MargotStarbuck.com.

Discover more resources
and join the community at:

Join the conversation…

#thesolidplace

Made in the USA
Columbia, SC
13 January 2019